Intersections:
Where Faith and Life Meet

*A Cumberland Presbyterian
Adult Resource
Volume 15, Advent/Christmas*

Discipleship Ministry Team
Ministry Council
Cumberland Presbyterian Church

8207 Traditional Place
Cordova, Tennessee 38016

© 2016 Discipleship Ministry Team

All Rights Reserved. No part of this book may be reproduced or transmitted in any form or by any means, electronic or mechanical, including photocopying, recording, or by any information storage or retrieval system, without permission in writing from the publisher. For information contact Discipleship Ministry Team, Cumberland Presbyterian Center, 8207 Traditional Place, Cordova, Tennessee, 38016-7414.

First Edition 2016

Published by The Discipleship Ministry Team
General Assembly Ministry Council of the Cumberland Presbyterian Church
Cordova, Tennessee

ISBN-13: 978-0692566268
ISBN-10: 0692566260

We want to hear from you.
Please send your comments about this curriculum to
the Discipleship Ministry Team at chm@cumberland.org.

OUR UNITED OUTREACH
Made Possible In Part By Your Tithe To Our United Outreach

Table of Contents

Lesson 1 New Life from Nowhere..4

Lesson 2 Could This Be a Sign?..13

Lesson 3 Comfort in the Desert..22

Lesson 4 A Righteous Branch...31

Lesson 5 Ancestry: What's in a Name?...40

Lesson 6 You Want Me to Do What?...50

Unless otherwise specified, all scripture text is from the New Revised Standard Version Bible, copyright 1989, Division of Christian Education of the National Council of the Churches of Christ in the United States of America. Used by permission. All rights reserved.

Editor: Cindy Martin
Proofreader: Pam Campbell

To order, call 901-276-4572, x 252 or e-mail resources@cumberland.org.

New Life From Nowhere

Scripture for lesson: Isaiah 11:1-7

Written by Chris Warren

A few years ago my family and I moved into a new home. We love our house and feel very fortunate to be a part of the neighborhood where we live. I enjoy doing things around the house, taking care of the yard, planting flowers, and trimming the trees.

Sometimes when I garden, however, I come across a plant that I don't want in the yard. No matter what I do, it just won't die. Even after cutting down it down, another new shoot appears.

The passage from Isaiah presents us with quite the opposite thought about a shoot from what was thought to be dead. In the case of God's continued love coming out of the stump of the tree of Jesse, we can find hope for newness of life and fellowship with God.

Prep for the Journey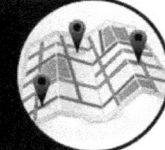

Isaiah is one of the most important prophets in all of scripture. Although scholars debate as to when Isaiah lived, how many people wrote under the name Isaiah, and when they wrote, the first several chapters of Isaiah are thought to have been written in Jerusalem between 742 BCE and about 700 BCE. So, as we deal with messianic prophecy that is fulfilled in Jesus, we have to remember that Isaiah was writing about 700 years before the birth of Jesus.

It is incredible to think that as Isaiah was watching the end of the Northern Kingdom (Israel) and probably concerned about the future of the Southern Kingdom (Judah), he was already looking ahead to a time when, out of that seemingly destroyed tree, a new shoot would begin to grow.

Read Isaiah 11:1.
A shoot shall come out from the stump of Jesse,
    and a branch shall grow out of his roots.

Sidebar questions:

What have you thought was dead only to see new life emerge? What feelings did you experience as a result?

How does realizing the time frame during which Isaiah wrote affect your understanding of his prophecy?

What gives you hope for a brighter future?

At the time Isaiah wrote, both kingdoms still existed, but Israel was in a precarious situation. Isaiah believed in God's sovereignty and that God would not allow the Davidic monarchy to fall. A new branch would not grow from the tree, but a new shoot would come from the stump.

The people of Israel were going to be cut off. It was going to seem as if they were gone. But it is important to remember that this new shoot would come from the life of the ancient Israelites. It was from Abraham, through Isaac, through Jacob. It was through Moses and Aaron. It was through the people who were enslaved and then became a nation. Although that nation was cut off, this new shoot would grow from a tree that had seemed dead; it would be a new thing out of the old, a new tree that would never be cut off again.

> When have you experienced the closure of a chapter in your life that later brought a new possibility? How has that experience changed your perspective?

On the Road

Isaiah's prophecy called people to imagine the future, to imagine what this new shoot would be like. Remember that this new shoot was to come from the stump of Jesse, who was David's father. In other words, this new shoot would continue in the line established by David. Yet by referencing David's father instead of David as the "stump," we may imagine that the shoot would supersede even David, who was lauded as the greatest ruler of Israel.

> Who are consider some of the modern world's great leaders? What qualities set them apart? How are those qualities reflective of Isaiah's prophecy?

Read Isaiah 11:2-3a.
The spirit of the Lord shall rest on him,
   the spirit of wisdom and understanding,
   the spirit of counsel and might,
   the spirit of knowledge and the fear of the Lord.
³ His delight shall be in the fear of the Lord.

For many of us, these words are well known. Every year as we celebrate Advent, we read or hear these words. Sometimes they are part of the scripture reading in worship, and sometimes we hear them in song. At other times we may not hear or read the actual words, but the images are forever in our minds as we contemplate what Jesus the Christ will be like when he returns to our world.

We celebrate Christmas knowing that Jesus is here. He is the righteous one. He is the embodiment of the Spirit of the Lord. He is wise and understands all things. He is mighty, and he knows and understands God intimately. There is none like Christ.

> In what ways do you see Jesus as having the spirit of understanding and wisdom?

As we read these words, we think not only of Christ in the manger, but of Jesus as he sat in the Temple and debated the priests while still a boy. We think of Jesus who called and taught disciples a new type of wisdom, a new type of relationship with God. We think of a Jesus whose obedience to God overcame even his fear and revulsion at the thought of his own death. We think of the Christ whom Isaiah described 700 years before his birth, and we realize that these words still ring true more than 2,000 years after his death.

Scenic Route

Read Isaiah 11:3b-5.
He shall not judge by what his eyes see,
  or decide by what his ears hear;
⁴ but with righteousness he shall judge the poor,
  and decide with equity for the meek of the earth;
he shall strike the earth with the rod of his mouth,
  and with the breath of his lips he shall kill the wicked.
⁵ Righteousness shall be the belt around his waist,
  and faithfulness the belt around his loins.

You might want to re-read that scripture. While the first section sounds like the way we think of Jesus, the second section seems a little bit different. If we look at it closely, it may seem just a little bit scary.

What does it mean that this new, righteous shoot will not judge by what he sees or hears? Just what criteria will this person use to judge? The answer is not given, but one possibility is to recall the words when God chose David to become king over Israel. Samuel had gone to anoint one of Jesse's sons to be the next king. He was confused when God passed by the good-looking, seemingly perfect candidates. God spoke to Samuel, "Do not look on his appearance or on the height of his stature, because I have rejected him; for the LORD does not see as mortals see; they look on the outward appearance, but the LORD looks on the heart" (1 Samuel 16:7).

So, perhaps the Messiah would judge by the heart instead of outward sight or sound, but what of the next section? The Christ will "judge the poor and decide with equity for the meek of the earth." I know that many times when we look at the extremely rich or famous, we may feel as if we are poor. But chances are, if you are reading this, you are in the richest class of people in the world. Having a roof over your head and food to eat is not standard in this world. According to www.globalissues.org, almost half the world lives on less than $2.50 per day. Over 80 percent of the world lives on less than $10 per day. For most of us, those figures put our own wealth in perspective.

If Christ is going to decide with equity for the meek of the earth, what will it mean for those who really aren't meek? We may need to contemplate this perspective as we read this passage.

When have you lost sight of the hope for wisdom and understanding in the world? What helps you to regain that hope?

By what criteria do you judge people? What criteria do people use to judge you?

What determines wealth in your life? In what situations might a rich person also be poor?

How does Jesus expect us to carry forth his work of judging the meek with equity?

Finally, scripture says that the Christ will "strike the earth with the rod of his mouth, and with the breath of his lips he shall kill the wicked." Wait a minute. This doesn't sound like the kind and gentle Jesus that we expect. It doesn't sound like the Jesus about whom we sing in the hymn "What a Friend We Have...." How do we make sense of this seemingly violent turn of phrase?

Perhaps when Jesus strikes the earth with the rod of his mouth, he is really telling us how we should live. Jesus said lots of things about how we should care for one another, what our top priorities should be, and what we should do to care for the poor. Those words were like striking the earth because they were supposed to shake up people and cause them to be different. They were to make people change.

But have we? Are those who are poor on our minds? Is God our number one priority? Do we live the Great Commandment? If we have heard the words and choose to ignore them or make excuses to be faithful later, does that make us the "wicked"? I believe it is something we have to think about in our own lives.

> In what ways do any of these descriptions of Jesus seem strange to you? How do you reconcile these descriptions with the first part of Isaiah's prophecy?

> How can we strive to be the righteous and avoid being the "wicked"?

Workers Ahead

What are we to do with Isaiah's words today? The text of Isaiah, ancient as it is, is not only a text for generations ago. It relates to us today, guiding us, informing us, and perhaps even warning us. It may have told the ancient people of Israel what to expect from the Messiah, but it can also inform us what the Messiah may be expecting from us.

Read Isaiah 11:6-7.

The wolf shall live with the lamb,
  the leopard shall lie down with the kid,
the calf and the lion and the fatling together,
  and a little child shall lead them.
⁷ The cow and the bear shall graze,
  their young shall lie down together;
  and the lion shall eat straw like the ox.

These verses are a vision of perfect peace for the future. In hindsight, we tend to regard the first part of this passage as separate from this part. The first part tells about the coming of the Christ, which Christians believe has already happened. But these words are about a future that has yet to be realized. When will these things happen? When will there be perfect peace?

For some, perfect peace is only in the future that comes after Jesus has returned to the earth. These scenes seem impossible in the present world, and many feel there is no hope of working toward such a

> As Christmas approaches, what changes in the world do you look forward to?

world without an entire re-making of the heavens and earth that can only God can do. From this mindset, there is little we can do in the present except await the perfect future.

But I believe God wants us to work toward a peaceful world now—one of peace, understanding, and cooperation. I am writing this lesson in the midst of the 2016 United States presidential race. The rhetoric that I hear is not only lacking any semblance of peace; some of it is downright vicious. We are all humans, all created by God in God's image. I believe humans are advanced enough to learn how to communicate without spouting hatred, false accusations, or prejudice. To paraphrase Mahatma Gandhi, we should be the change we want to see in the world.

If we want better dialogue, we have to engage in better dialogue. If we want an end to poverty, we have to work toward that end. If we want peace between nations, we need to seek peace in our own lives—between ourselves and our friends and family members.

Peace can exist even if we have different opinions. Surely the lion and the lamb don't agree on everything, but in God's visions of the perfect future, they co-exist. Humanity can do this, too.

In the Rear View

Isaiah prophesied over 2,700 years ago, but he gave us a promise that we celebrate at least every Advent season, and probably many times throughout the year. The promise was for a good and wise shepherd who would come and care for us. But the promise was also one of righteous judgment.

As we move toward the Christmas season, it is wonderful to celebrate the birth of the Savior. It is beautiful to imagine the innocent baby wrapped in swaddling clothes and lying in the manger. It is inspiring to hear the story of Mary and Joseph and how they came to be the caretakers of the Messiah.

But we must also look to the requirements of being followers of Jesus. What did Jesus ask of us? How should we live if we are to follow Jesus faithfully? Even a short prophecy about the coming of a shoot from the stump of Jesse written 700 years before Jesus' birth can challenge the way we live today, if we allow it.

> How can you work for peace in your life? your workplace? your church? your home?
>
> How can you change the perceptions of others that lead to anger, strife, and violence?
>
> How are you celebrating God's promise? In what ways do you see that promise being fulfilled?
>
> How have you fulfilled the requirements of a follower of Jesus? Where might you still have some work to do?

Travel Log

Day 1:

It can be difficult to take time out of our busy lives to contemplate the place that faith in Jesus has in our lives. When we look back at Isaiah's writing, we are impressed that so many years before his arrival, the people were interested in, perhaps even obsessed with, the coming of a Messiah. What does the coming of the Messiah mean to you? How does Jesus' entry into the world change who you are? Take a moment to write about how you are changed by the good news of Jesus.

Day 2:

Isaiah wrote that the Messiah's delight would be the "fear of the Lord." We do not tend to think that this meant being afraid of God, but more an awesome respect of who God is.

Without screening your answers, take a moment to respond in writing to the following questions: How do you need to remind yourself about "fear of the Lord"? What does it look like in your life? How could remembering that Jesus himself would delight in "fear of the Lord" change your perception of that fear in your life?

Day 3:

Scripture tells us that Jesus will not judge by what he sees or hears. How do you make sense of this statement? How do you tend to judge your world, your surroundings, other people, or even yourself? Do you judge by what you see and hear? Do you judge by something else?

Write down some ways that you make judgments based on outward appearance. Then write down ways that you want to judge others--perhaps by learning about their minds and hearts, or by setting aside any pre-conceptions you might have based on sight alone.

Day 4:

"Equity for the poor..." Who are the poor in the world? In the lesson there were some brief statistics about income, but is poverty judged solely by income level? What are some other factors?

How can you identify someone who is poor and give of yourself so he or she may become enriched? Or, how can you work together with fellow believers to solve a need in your community or the world?

Write down some of the groups of people in your area of the world who are poor. What organizations are caring for them? Pray for these organizations and their work in the world. Become involved with their work by volunteering or making a donation.

Day 5:

A peaceful world sounds so good and inviting, but it seems so difficult to achieve. We engage in conflicts every day. If we follow politics, we may lose our cool when defending our own position. Something as simple as a small misunderstanding within our family can also lead to strife. How can we live out the words of St. Francis who said, "Lord, make me an instrument of your peace"?

Take a moment to journal about what peace in the world would look like to you and how you can be an instrument of peace.

Day 6:

The Israelites' expected the Christ to come and retake their land and reign over them as a righteous king. We know that Jesus came in a different way than was anticipated. What do you expect Jesus to do in the world? Describe how your expectations are biblically based. Do you expect something from Jesus that God may not have intended? Take a few moment to list your expectations.

Day 7:

As Isaiah looked forward to the coming of the Messiah, he saw that the earth would be radically changed. Some of these things have already come to be, and some we still await. What responsibility does a follower of Christ have to work toward a day of peace?

Write down some achievable goals that you can work toward. Use those goals to remind you how to advocate differences in our world.

Could This Be a Sign?

Scripture for Lesson: Isaiah 7:10-14

Written by Chris Warren

There is a great scene toward the beginning of the film *Bruce Almighty* in which the main character, Bruce, is having an especially bad day, and he takes his frustration out on God. Bruce runs out of his house and starts driving down the highway, asking God to help him. He admits he is desperate, and he asks God for answers, specifically asking time and time again for a sign, any sign, that God is there and that God can do something about his situation.

As he drives along, a road sign flashes "Caution Ahead." Not noticing that sign, Bruce asks for another sign. A truck pulls in front of him, carrying hundreds of road signs in the back. Who says God doesn't have a sense of humor (at least in the opinion of the filmmakers)?

This lesson is about signs. Sometimes we can see them clearly, and sometimes, like Bruce, they are right in front of us, but we miss them. Isaiah wrote about things to come so that the people would recognize them, but not everyone was able or willing to see those signs.

Prep for the Journey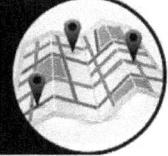

As we explored in the first session of this series, the first forty or so chapters of the Book of Isaiah were written between approximately 742 BCE and 700 BCE, which were difficult times for the people of Israel. The kingdom had been divided for many years, and there were separate rulers in the north and the south. But in the time when chapter 7 was written, the kingdoms were at a low point in their relations. The Southern kingdom, Judah, was preparing for an attack from the Northern kingdom, Israel. The Northern king was not coming alone to attack the Southern kingdom. He had joined the king of Damascus in an anti-Assyrian coalition that was coming to fight Judah. Their plan was to take the throne from King Ahaz and put a king on the throne who would join their coalition.

> When have you asked for or received a sign from God? How easy was it to recognize the sign?

> What low points have you experienced personally? as part of a group? Where did you turn for support?

> How can you tell when you are being called to have greater faith or when you are being called to ask for help?

> When have you faced an obstacle that seemed overwhelming? How has such a situation tested your faith? How did you respond?

> What helps you to understand the signs in your own life?

Isaiah was fiercely against joining any coalition, whether it was one against their enemies to the North, which would have meant joining with the Assyrians, or a coalition against the Assyrians, who were poised to take over the Northern kingdom and much of the known world. Isaiah insisted that the people didn't need outside help to protect Judah; they didn't need another army to help them protect the capital city of Jerusalem. What they needed, according to Isaiah, was more faith.

As we come to the scripture we will be studying today, we need to know that King Ahaz had pretty much made up his mind to join the Assyrians as a vassal nation so that his kingdom would have protection from the coalition that was forming against Judah. Isaiah strongly argued against this decision in the verses preceding today's lesson. The prophecy that begins in verse 10 is a continuation of Isaiah's argument with King Ahaz about asking for protection from the Assyrians.

On the Road

Signs from God seem to be notoriously difficult to interpret. At least they seem so in our modern world. Any unusual occurrence may be cited as a sign from God by many, and each of those citing that occurrence will likely have a different opinion as to what that sign might mean.

In the past few years people have named several different dates as the final day of the world's existence. Just a few years ago, a business owner in the town where I was living advertised that he was selling all his equipment and that his business would be closed on a certain date due to the end of days. I don't mean to make light of the situation; many people sincerely believed that they had correctly interpreted the signs they had received.

Read Isaiah 7:10-13.

Again the LORD spoke to Ahaz, saying, ¹¹ Ask a sign of the LORD your God; let it be deep as Sheol or high as heaven. ¹² But Ahaz said, I will not ask, and I will not put the LORD to the test. ¹³ Then Isaiah said: "Hear then, O house of David! Is it too little for you to weary mortals, that you weary my God also?

As I read this passage, I immediately thought of Jesus' response on the pinnacle of the Temple. (See Matthew 4:5-7.) It seems reasonable that the king would respond in just the way he did. Of course you should not put the LORD your God to the test. It is clearly in the law.

Then again, if we read the passage closely, we will see that it was the LORD who invited Ahaz to ask for a sign in the first place. I learned once that sin is a deviation from what God expects or wants someone to do. In this case, God specifically told Ahaz what to do, and Ahaz disobeyed.

Isaiah's response hints at a reason. Ahaz had already decided what he wanted to do—ally Judah with the Assyrians, whether Isaiah or even God wanted him to do so or not. Ahaz was supposed to ask for a sign to confirm what God wanted, but he was unwilling to ask for a sign that might not give him the answer he sought. So, Isaiah says, God will give him a sign whether he asks for it or not.

> When have you wanted to walk your own path, even if you knew that it was not the right one?
>
> When have you avoided asking God for confirmation about something, or continued to ask God for another answer when you had already received an answer, just one you didn't want?

Scenic Route

Prophecy is sometimes thought of as foretelling the distant future, but for much of the prophecy in our scripture, it was telling of events that were in the near future. Within the context of the chapter, it appears that God intended to give Ahaz a sign to prove the truth of Isaiah's words.

Read Isaiah 7:14.
Therefore the Lord himself will give you a sign. Look, the young woman is with child and shall bear a son, and shall name him Immanuel.

Many of us have grown up hearing the words in this portion of Isaiah's prophecy all our lives. For several years I was a part of a performance of Handel's *Messiah* every Christmas. The words of this prophecy, from the King James Version of the Bible, are etched in my memory from one of those pieces of music. Here's the way I remember it from the KJV: "Behold, a virgin shall conceive, and bear a son, and shall call his name Immanuel."

Doubtless many of you will be surprised by the NRSV translation of this passage. The word virgin is nowhere to be found. The word used here is a cognate of the Hebrew word *'almâh*, which means "young woman/maiden." According to the *New Interpreter's Bible Commentary*, this word has no connotations about the marital or sexual status of the woman. Modern Bible scholars think that the young woman in the prophecy likely was Isaiah's wife or Judah's queen. Before the child is roughly two years old, the Northern kingdom will have been defeated. The sign was soon in coming, soon enough to teach the king of Judah about his own future.

When the Hebrew Bible was translated into Greek, the word gained the meaning of virgin. That translation was called the Septuagint, and it was completed sometime in the third century, BCE.

God can use things in ways that we do not begin to understand. Many prophecies, especially in the Book of Isaiah, have been used

> How does the idea that the passage referred to a woman in Isaiah's time surprise you? What interests or troubles you about that idea?

to tell of a coming Messiah. We believe that Jesus is the fulfillment of those prophecies and the one who came into the world, the very Christ. The words of Isaiah can refer not only to a prophecy for his day, but also to the coming of one who will fulfill the name that was spoken of him, *Immanuel*, which means "God with us."

These words have become a part of our understanding of the expectation of a coming Messiah for the Jewish people. By the time the Gospels were written, the Septuagint was available and would have been studied for clues as to the coming of Jesus. Those who studied the scriptures found many references like this one. While they likely would have affirmed the commonly held meaning within the text, they further applied it to the birth of Jesus the Christ.

Workers Ahead

Some Christians have had a hard time with the concept discussed here. They point to other important figures throughout history who claimed also to have been born of a virgin. In my research for this lesson, I learned that approximately one percent of mothers in the United States claim to have had a child as a virgin.

The prophecies of Isaiah have instilled faith in many people since long before the birth of Jesus. Our understanding of ourselves and of our Savior have been shaped by those prophecies and the ways they are explained and discussed in the New Testament. Some Christians insist that there must be no deviation on such a foundational part of Christian doctrine, but other Christians claim that the essentials of who Christ was, what Christ did, and how Christ atoned for the world are unaffected by the issue of a virgin birth.

It is not my plan to choose one path or another. I leave that up to the reader, and expect that it will be an interesting topic of discussion for the group. As your group has this discussion, remember that some members may have a very strong belief one way or the other. It is my hope that nothing I have presented here will cause discord or argument, just healthy discussion.

The prophecies of Isaiah continue to inspire us in the modern world. We read something Isaiah wrote around 2,700 years ago, and we see it fulfilled in our faith over 2,000 years later. Learning from Isaiah about the coming of the Messiah gives us perspective on our faith. It allows us to look at the story of the people of God not as something that has already happened, but as something that continues to happen. The story we are living is part of the story about which Isaiah wrote so many years ago. The story of our faith today connects to the story of Jesus the baby, Jesus the man, Jesus the teacher, and Jesus the Christ.

How do you understand the virgin birth? How might you explain it to someone who was unfamiliar with Christianity?

How does the way you understand the virgin birth affect you as a believer?

How do you feel about the idea that the story of God's people is continuing to happen? What is your role in that story? the role of your community of faith?

God continues to do new things. That thread has run through the story we have in the Bible, and it has continued through time. Placing our lives into that story is part of what we receive when we look at scripture as the continuing journey of humankind back into God's arms.

> What new things is God doing in your life? in your faith community? What signs of these new things have you seen?

In the Rear View

In the midst of a difficult time in the life of the Southern kingdom of Judah, God called Isaiah to tell the king what God wanted him to do. Isaiah prophesied that King Ahaz was to trust only in God and not in foreign armies to save the people. At this time in history, Isaiah's words saved the people, but just over one hundred years later another king would hear from another prophet, Jeremiah, who would say much the same thing. This time, however, the king would not listen, and, much like the Northern kingdom in Isaiah's time, the Southern kingdom fell. The people were taken into captivity.

We are to take seriously the prophecies, many of which were written down during the Babylonian Exile, as they inform our present day faith. We can both affirm the meaning that the prophecy likely had for its first audience, the king and the people in Isaiah's time, while we continuing to affirm the way those prophecies point to something else, namely, the birth of Jesus the Messiah.

It is OK to be Christian and still have questions about some of the things that the Church has taught through the centuries. The idea of a virgin birth is exciting, inspiring, amazing, and difficult—maybe even all of these things at the same time. Wrestling with these matters is not a sign of lack of faith. It could even be seen as a depth of faith.

> How has the information in this lesson changed your way of thinking? How has it deepened your faith?

Travel Log

Day 1:
   Take a moment to think of an adversary or an obstacle in your life about which you are concerned. Ahaz had invading armies. Maybe it seems to you that invading armies are threatening your life. How can you heed Isaiah's advice and look only to the Lord? Write a prayer asking for faith to trust in God in the face of this obstacle.

Day 2:
   Who in your life is speaking the word of the Lord to you? Maybe it is a friend, a spouse, or other family member. Maybe it is someone you have never met but who has written something inspiring or who lives in a way that you admire. What is God trying to tell you through that person? How are you going to allow that message to permeate your life?
   If you know of someone who speaks God's word to you, write his or her name in the space below. Then write words you imagine this person would say to you. If you cannot think of someone, use Isaiah as your prophet. What message would God give to Isaiah for you?

Day 3:

God encouraged Ahaz to ask for a sign. God said it should be a sign as deep as the underworld or as high as heaven above. Sometimes we wait for signs, but they don't seem to come. Other times, when we look back on our lives, we can see signs that should have been plain as day, but we missed them in the middle of our struggle. Write about a time such as that in your life. When was there a clear sign from God? In what ways might you have been trying to avoid it? How might God be giving you a sign today? What would help you to recognize it?

Day 4:

Think of the "young woman" in the passage from Isaiah 7. Remember biblical scholars suggest that in Isaiah's time, the young woman was either the wife of Isaiah or the wife of King Ahaz. Imagine what her life must have been like. How might she have felt about being a "sign from God?" Write about how you might feel if God were to use you as a sign in someone else's life.

Day 5:
During the season of Advent we focus on the events that led up to the birth of Jesus. The life and gifts of Mary are some of the greatest parts of this story. Take some time today to think about Mary. Who was she? What must her life have been like? How could she have faced her society, unmarried and pregnant? Imagine her shame.

Write down some groups of people that experience shame in our world. How can you minister to them?

Day 6:
Our perception of many things changes as we get older. I think very differently about the story of Mary now that I have a daughter who is likely about the same age as Mary when she was engaged and while she carried the Christ Child. How has your perception of Mary and her story changed over the years? Write a letter to Mary. What would you like to talk about with her if you had the chance?

Day 7:
This lesson has had some interesting and perhaps challenging information. Take some time to write down what you might want to explore related to this lesson. What things in your walk of faith are non-negotiable? What things do you wonder about or even question?

Comfort in the Desert

Scripture for lesson: Isaiah 40:1-5

Written by Whitney Brown

I was eighteen years old, and it was three days before Christmas when the phone rang with news that my childhood best friend had died. In that instant, a season that is marked by light and hope, love, joy, and peace became dark and cold. Even surrounded by friends and family, the world had never felt lonelier. God seemed so far away. Just a few short weeks after affirming my call to ministry, everything seemed to disappear. My life had seemingly just begun to flourish and grow when my heart became like a desert.

Those feelings lasted for a long time. Seasons in the desert seem slow to change. While we can't force ourselves out of such seasons, we can decide how to spend our long wait. No matter how dark the world seemed or how far away I felt from God, I knew God remained near, and that the light would eventually overcome the darkness. Such promises move us to hopeful action, even in our desert places.

Prep for the Journey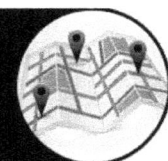

In the previous lesson, Isaiah was offering hope to the divided kingdoms—Judah and Israel. By this point, both kingdoms had fallen to the invading armies of the Assyrians or the Babylonians. Whereas the earlier chapters of Isaiah were written in the mid- to early seventh century BCE, the second half of this book is thought to have been written in the mid-sixth century BCE. By this time the people had been living in exile for a long time and were feeling hopeless.

Because many of their worship practices had become central to the Temple in Jerusalem, it was even difficult for the people to feel connected to their faith. They could not go to the Temple to offer sacrifices or to observe the high holy days and feasts that had become such an important part of their lives. The Temple was seen as God's dwelling place, which meant that the people even felt disconnected from God.

What desert places have you experienced in your life? How did you feel God's promises?

What type of exiles have you experienced? How did they affect you? What gave you hope during those times?

What helps you to feel connected to your faith?

The prophet Isaiah spoke words of comfort and encouragement to the people of Jerusalem (a metaphor for all of God's people). How barren the world must have felt to them before they heard Isaiah's words.

Read Isaiah 40:1-2.
Comfort, O comfort my people,
  says your God.
² Speak tenderly to Jerusalem,
  and cry to her
that she has served her term,
  that her penalty is paid,
that she has received from the LORD's hand
  double for all her sins.

God's people had lived under years of unjust rule at home and then watched as foreign armies invaded their country. They had been separated from all that was their own and were living as a people without a place—unable to be the community they were called to be.

The people of Israel and Judah had known God's presence, and they had also felt the weight of the consequences of their unfaithfulness. Now they were not even able to approach the places where they had once felt that God was near. In their exile, could God, would God come near to them? Amidst such brokenness in their physical world, in their spiritual world, and in their own hearts, would the Lord still hear their cries? Would God still deliver those who would dare to follow? It was to those who asked such questions that Isaiah spoke these words of comfort, reminding them that God was near.

On the Road

Even in our desert places, those most barren places of our hearts and lives, God still forgives and comforts. We know that God is always near. We can trust that promise, even when nothing else seems right in the world.

But God doesn't stop there. Not only does God stay near to us in comfort, but God also continues to call us, even in the desert places. God still calls us to the work of being disciples. Isaiah reassured the people of God's comfort, but he also reminded them that their work was far from finished.

The words given to Isaiah are a call to be in solidarity with those who are suffering. Comfort them. Speak to them. Cry with them. This is empathy—not judgment nor sympathy. Judgment would supply a list of wrongs, which would no doubt be long for the unfaithful and

---

How do you offer comfort to God's people? In what ways have you received comfort?

When has God seemed to be far away? When have you felt disconnected from God?

What does it mean to you that God is near, even when you feel disconnected from God? How can you share that promise with someone who needs to hear it today?

To what work is God calling you? How are you responding to God's call?

Whom do you know who is suffering? How are you being in solidarity with them?

neglectful people of Israel. There were times when God supplied them with such a list and told them how to turn from their unfaithfulness, but this passage is different. Sympathy looks upon and points to suffering, but remains disconnected. The comfort sympathy offers does not reach the heart of suffering because it does not involve self-giving. Empathy requires putting ourselves in the mess with those who are suffering. The comfort God offers is empathetic because God is present in the desert, in the chaos, in times of suffering. This call, issued by God through Isaiah, is for all who would hear it to be truly present with those who are suffering. In so doing, we add a little healing to the brokenness of our sacred community.

> When have you felt the difference between sympathy and empathy? How are you able to offer empathy to others?

Read Isaiah 40:3-4.
A voice cries out:
"In the wilderness prepare the way of the LORD,
*   make straight in the desert a highway for our God.*
⁴ Every valley shall be lifted up,
*   and every mountain and hill be made low;*
the uneven ground shall become level,
*   and the rough places a plain.*

Isaiah spoke God's words to a people with a very murky history. Their ancestors, barely out of the gates of slavery in Egypt, began to forge false idols to save themselves from impending doom, not trusting the God they knew to deliver, to do what had been promised. This mistrust has been repeated throughout their history—and our own. Though God has always been faithful, it can be hard to see past the current circumstances. Feeling that God was far from them, the promises of a Messiah forgotten, the people had stopped preparing the way.

> Why was it necessary to prepare the way for the Messiah? How do Christians today need to continue to prepare the way?

Advent is a time of remembrance and preparation. We remember the story of creation—how God took the most dark, formless chaos and brought structure and life and purpose. We remember that God has always called that creation back to goodness and purpose, even when it has wandered far from its roots. We remember the stories of Israel, the promise of a Messiah who would deliver them even in the midst of their greatest suffering. We remember that God never stopped sending prophets to call the people back to their work of preparation for the Messiah and the Kingdom that was coming. We remember how God answered centuries of cries more fully than anyone could have ever imagined through a refugee baby born among livestock. God continued to prepare the way, even when God's people missed the whole heart of God's covenants.

> Why was/is a Messiah needed? How are you and your faith community "preparing the way" this Advent?

> What do you believe is at the heart of all God's covenants?

Scenic Route

Isaiah 40:3 is referenced in the New Testament, pointing to John the Baptist as the one in the wilderness who would prepare the way for the Messiah, Jesus. The word *prepare* used here, and quoted in the New Testament in reference to John the Baptist, literally translated means one who goes out before a king's journey to level the way and make it passable. "The idea is taken from the practice of eastern monarchs, who, whenever they entered upon an expedition or took a journey, especially through desert and unpractised countries, sent harbingers before them to prepare all things for their passage, and pioneers to open the passes, to level the ways, and to remove all impediments" (https://www.studylight.org/commentaries/acc/isaiah-40.html#3 [October 25, 2016]).

We know from the infancy narratives shared this time of year that John the Baptist and Jesus were connected from the womb. John prepared the way for Christ from beginning to end. From a miraculous birth to a violent death, we can see the parallels in their stories. Before Jesus' public ministry, John was ministering and baptizing, proclaiming the Messiah's arrival. His followers included supporters and those who were resistant to his teachings. Because of John's preparation, he was immediately able to recognize the Messiah when Jesus stepped onto the scene.

We know from the life of Jesus and his earliest followers that living a life focused on God's kingdom is risky. God created the world from chaos. From this creation came beauty, growth, peace, and harmonious relationships among each unique piece of creation. Humanity was told to tend and care for it all, but that harmony was broken, and the brokenness continues each and every day. Cultures result from brokenness; systems and entire societies are built upon brokenness. To work toward making our world more like the promised kingdom, to do the work we are called to do, means dismantling the systems that result from brokenness. "Every valley shall be lifted up, every mountain and hill be made low." These are huge shifts, and we cannot expect them to be easy or comfortable, but we can trust that the work of preparing for them is our call.

What things do we need to make ready? What needs to be cleared or leveled so that there is an unobstructed way to God in our lives?

What is risky about living a life focused on God's kingdom? Why?

What systems are the result of brokenness? How is your faith community being called to restore those systems?

Workers Ahead

Read Isaiah 40:5.
*Then the glory of the Lord shall be revealed,
   and all people shall see it together,
   for the mouth of the Lord has spoken."*

The goal in all of this preparation is the glory of the Lord. The only way we achieve it is together, in community. When the beloved community of God is restored, the glory of the Lord will be revealed, and we will see it—together.

The brokenness is of our own making, but no amount of work can fix it apart from faithfulness to God and God's promises. God has never stopped working toward the reconciliation of creation, but we must do our part, and we must do it together. We can believe it will happen, and we can have hope because God speaks comfort in the chaos and promises to be present with us. We can be sure that we are called to work and be present with those who are suffering, to cry out with them. Once we have found ourselves amidst the brokenness, we must begin to prepare the way, level the path, work toward a world more like the kingdom God has promised. When we work together to bring about God's kingdom, light breaks through the darkness, and we begin to see the miraculous work of Christ in our hearts and in our world.

> In what areas of your life do you need to hear words of comfort? Where do you need to speak comfort?
>
> What is the uneven ground in need of leveling in your community? How can you answer the call to prepare the way in the wilderness?
>
> Determine a way to practice empathy in the places of brokenness you identified. Practice empathy this week, working among those who are clearing their way through the chaos.

In the Rear View

Have you had enough? Does the world feel heavy? The holidays are an especially hard time for many people. This prophecy carries a heavy challenge, but it begins with a word—comfort. While much of what follows does not sound like comfortable work, the refrain is the same—God will do it. God has done it. God is doing it. You will find what you need for today, and you will begin again tomorrow. You do your part, and know God is faithful to do the rest.

Share together what you have gathered from Isaiah's challenge. What is "your part" today?

Travel Log

Day 1:

Jot down some words that describe a time when you felt far from God, a desert place. How did God's comfort guide you as you worked your way through the brokenness?

Day 2:

Focus on the meaning of Advent. During this time we remember that the coming of the Messiah was the "first advent." The earliest hearers of Isaiah's prophecy were to be at work, preparing the way for the Messiah, even while in exile. We are now in the "second advent" as we await Christ's return. We are to be preparing for that which we pray, God's "kingdom come." How are you preparing the way for the transforming love of Christ in our world? Make some notes about what you can and will do.

Day 3:
   Reread Isaiah 40:1-5. What do you think these words meant to their original audience? What do they mean for you today? Journal your thoughts.

Day 4:
   Think of a time when you have been able to tell the difference between empathy and sympathy. Describe the event(s) and how you experienced the difference. Write a few words about how the responses made you feel.

Day 5:
Describe a time someone has cared for you in a time of need. Write that person a note of gratitude.

Day 6:
Describe a time you have cared for someone in his or her time of need. Who may need your care now?

Day 7:
Review what your group discussed in "Workers Ahead." What does your individual part of being present in the brokenness look like?

A Righteous Branch

Scripture for lesson: Jeremiah 23:5-6; Zechariah 6:12-13

Written by Whitney Brown

Have you ever done something you loved, practiced your particular gift, for no reason other than you love doing it? It's a good discipline to keep. As an artist, I have been fortunate to find a way to use my creative gifts in my work. However, by doing so I sometimes get caught up in the work, the need to complete something for a particular purpose, and I lose sight of why I love the process of creating.

I recently sat down at a blank canvas with an assortment of brushes and a colorful palette in front of me and absolutely no "reason" to paint. There was no end goal, no deadline, no real need for whatever would be produced. As I painted, layering colors and textures, pausing between layers, I remembered how much of the creative process occurs in this expectant, in-between stage of the work. Those moments of beautiful brush strokes and even the frustrating errors make the final piece worth seeing.

When we miss being present in the process, we have missed the journey. We expect the end result to be something beautiful and worth our time and effort, which is what drives us forward, yet what we do with that expectancy is just as important as what is to come.

> What does "being present in the process" mean to you?

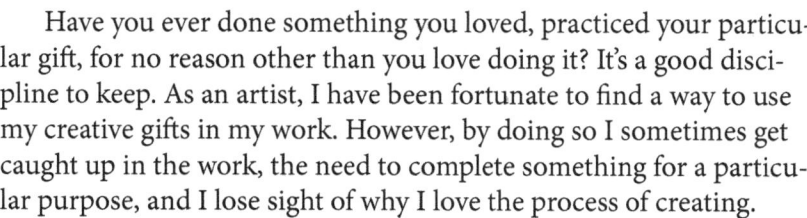

Prep for the Journey

As we look at the various words of prophecy that have come to be understood as foretelling the birth of the Messiah, we encounter another major prophet (Jeremiah) and one who was considered to be a minor prophet (Zechariah). Although these two men lived in different times and circumstances, their words for the people of Israel are very similar.

When the Babylonians destroyed Jerusalem, Jeremiah moved to Mizpah, which was where the newly appointed Jewish governor resided. After the governor's assassination, Jeremiah was deported

> What message might the prophets have for us today? How closely do you think those messages would parallel the ones of Jeremiah and Zechariah?

to Egypt by Jewish leaders. Obviously, they did not appreciate some of his words! But even in Egypt, Jeremiah continued to share God's messages.

Jeremiah spent a lot of time rebuking the people of Jerusalem, especially the leaders. He recounted the many ways they had been unfaithful to God and pronounced God's judgment upon them. However, while Jeremiah described the judgment as coming from the Lord, he made sure everyone understood that this discipline was the consequence of decades of bad leadership.

> Where do you see evidence of God's discipline today? How can we differentiate between God's discipline and events that occur naturally in the world?

Those who were supposed to lead and shepherd the people had exploited the ones in their care. They were unjust rulers, creating and reinforcing economic oppression upon those who were the most vulnerable. Jeremiah explained that God would deal with those who had neglected their duty to provide and care for the community. Their neglect had brought them to this mess, and they must live in it.

> What or who is being neglected in your community? How has that neglect created chaos?

Zechariah was called to be a prophet after Persia conquered Babylon. The Persian emperor, Cyrus the Great, allowed the Jewish exiles to return to Jerusalem, where they began to rebuild the destroyed city. Most important, they were allowed to rebuild the Temple. With the return to Jerusalem, the exiles could re-establish their religious, cultural, and social practices. As they begin to reconnect with their identity, Zechariah urged them to renew their covenant with God. Zechariah's time was one of restoration for God's people.

> What religious, social, and cultural practices need to be re-established? How has their demise affected you? your community of faith?

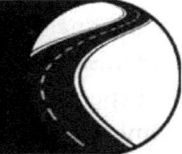

On the Road

Although Jeremiah focused on past and present judgment, he also proclaimed a future hope. God's last word is not wrath but grace. Something new is coming. Israel had failed to be faithful, failed to care for one another and practice justice and righteousness. The society had become built on oppression rather the beauty of the covenant community. However, God would raise up a leader who would bring reconciliation among the leaders and those they served, reconciliation among God and the people.

Zechariah emphasized the need for purification. While living in exile, the people had stopped observing the religious rituals that would have purified them in God's sight. They would also have been in regular contact with foreign gods. Their sin and ritual uncleanness would have made them unacceptable to God, also making their worship unacceptable.

> What does it mean to be purified in God's sight today? Do you think that your worship is ever unacceptable to God? Why or why not?

Both Jeremiah and Zechariah spoke of the Messiah as a "Branch,"—one who would come out of their community from the line of David to redeem all they had lost. The Messiah would bring justice, righteousness, and safety according to Jeremiah. Zechariah said he would restore the Temple, the honor of Jerusalem, and a peaceful community.

Read Jeremiah 23:5-6.

The days are surely coming, says the LORD, when I will raise up for David a righteous Branch, and he shall reign as king and deal wisely, and shall execute justice and righteousness in the land. ⁶ In his days Judah will be saved and Israel will live in safety. And this is the name by which he will be called: "The LORD is our righteousness."

Read Zechariah 6:12-13.

Thus says the LORD of hosts: Here is a man whose name is Branch: for he shall branch out in his place, and he shall build the temple of the LORD. ¹³ It is he that shall build the temple of the LORD; he shall bear royal honor, and shall sit upon his throne and rule. There shall be a priest by his throne, with peaceful understanding between the two of them.

Through centuries of waiting for a Messiah, Israel had developed some high expectations. During Advent, we reflect on what it's like to be in this time of expectation. Waiting is something with which we're all too familiar, and something many of us do not handle well. Waiting requires patience. Waiting requires trust. This type of Advent waiting requires something more; it requires action.

The church often tries to move too quickly through the season of Advent. We'd like to skip ahead to Christmas to make sure we get a few weeks to sing all our favorite carols and bask in the glory of the baby in the manger. But we must wait. If we do not wait, we miss the fullness to be found in the process.

We can experience joy in the time of waiting, the time of expectation. We must fully live in the process if we are to understand what to expect and not miss the fullness of what is coming. The journey, the expectation, the process is part of the whole. If you miss it, you have missed everything.

Jeremiah spoke to a people for whom that tangible hope still seemed a little out of reach. In exile, in the mess created by their unjust rulers, Jeremiah reminded them of God's faithfulness, but they couldn't quite see it yet. They were waiting for the space to dream. The Messiah must come and show them the way out of the mess.

Zechariah spoke to those who had the hope in their hands. Bricks and mortar for a new Temple lay before them, waiting to be used. The Messiah was surely coming, and the community must be ready.

How do you handle waiting?

What enables you to find joy in waiting? What unexpected blessings have you received as a result of waiting?

Where are you in this process of hopeful expectation? Does hope still seem intangible, or have you begun rebuilding?

Scenic Route

Advent is about rejoicing in what is coming, but also the process of getting there. It's like a rehearsal during which we train our hearts to be present in the waiting so they will be ready and fully present for what is to come.

When actors rehearse, they may first begin by simply reading the script, but when it's really time to begin, they go to the stage where they use the movements, tones, and rhythms that bring the story to life. It's a process of finding just the right balance of emotion, action, and pause. The process of rehearsing is as much a part of being an actor as the long-awaited performance.

The same is true for an athlete. Through practice one develops the habits and skills necessary to do his or her best work.

As Israel waited for a Messiah, as the prophets proclaimed his coming, the people's expectations grew. When the people followed that expectation to being active participants in the waiting—when they walked and moved about the world with the confidence of a people of promise, a people called to follow a just and righteous leader—they were using their wait well.

For Jeremiah's audience, even though their hope seemed to be in an unforeseeable future, they heard the promise of a ruler, a Messiah, who would change everything. Unlike the injustice with which they had lived for centuries, the new rule would be one of righteousness and justice. The community would be reconciled as those who had been pushed to the bottom were restored. Instead of passively waiting for the Messiah, they needed to begin to live into this prophecy—seeking the justice and righteousness of which they dreamed, becoming the beloved community they hoped to embody, pursuing the covenantal love God had promised to them.

Those to whom Zechariah spoke were laboring. "If we build it, they will come!" If we rebuild Jerusalem and the Temple, the Messiah will come! Their hard labor was the easy part. They were also in the process of rebuilding their identity, renewing their covenant with God, and remembering how to care for one another.

In this, the second advent, as we await Christ's return, dream of a world more like the kingdom, build our identity as individuals and as a covenantal community, what do Jeremiah and Zechariah say to us?

What are your expectations during this season of Advent?

What is necessary for reconciliation and restoration to occur?

Where is your labor focused? How are your efforts renewing hope and caring for others?

Workers Ahead

If we truly believe Christ was this promised leader of wisdom and justice, and if we still expect God to move and create in the world as has always been promised, then we must also move with the expectation of being the type of people worthy of these promises.

Our expectation requires us to share our gifts for the good of the community, to bare our souls and our needs to those in our lives. We fulfill our call, we experience the fullness of our expectation when we do so in community.

For both Jeremiah and Zechariah, the care of the community was central to the people's return to faithfulness and preparation for the Messiah. Between now and the next time your group gathers, determine needs within your surrounding community. Find the places where needs are not being met or identify organizations/groups that meet needs about which you feel passionate. Be prepared to share your ideas with others in your group. Choose a way to be involved in meeting that need or partnering with that organization throughout the coming year.

> How do you share your gifts for the good of the community? What keeps you from baring your soul and sharing your needs with those who are in your life?

In the Rear View

We are in a "second advent." Much like ancient Israel, we are waiting. The world around and within us often seems much closer to chaos than the kingdom we have been promised. These ancient prophecies were fulfilled in Jesus, yet God is still working in the world to bring reconciliation. Jesus has promised to return. We pray, "your kingdom come," believing that a new and better rule is ahead. We move and work in the world because something new and better is still coming, and we are called to be a part of it. What we do each day, in the process of this coming kingdom, is valuable. May we be present in the process.

Travel Log

Day 1:

Jesus fulfilled these Old Testament prophecies in both expected and unexpected ways. How did Jesus live into what Israel believed God had promised? How did Jesus fulfill the prophecies beyond those expectations? Record your responses in the space below.

Day 2:

How can we apply what we learn from the expected/unexpected fulfillments within the first advent as we actively wait today? Write down some of your thoughts.

Day 3:

Revisit "Workers Ahead." Begin to make the list of needs you would like to address or organizations you would like your group to connect with in the coming year. Consider why those needs are important to you. Add to this list throughout the week.

Day 4:

Reread the verses from Jeremiah and Zechariah. What do these prophecies say to you today? Journal your thoughts in the space below.

Day 5:

What are your expectations for the season of Advent? How will you use this season to glorify the birth of Jesus? the surpassing greatness of God? Make some notes in the space provided.

Day 6:

Plan to do something that you enjoy but that requires preparation (painting, cooking, exercising, gardening). Describe your experience of being present in the process.

Day 7:
Consider the metaphor of the "Branch." What meaning does it hold for you? As you ponder this question, doodle, draw, or write your responses below.

Ancestry: What's in a Name?

Scripture for lesson: Matthew 1:1-17

Written by Chris Warren

Last year I did something I have been intending to do for a long time. I got a membership to a genealogy website and started researching my family. Going through records, trying to figure out just which ones are accurate and which ones are dead ends is a tedious process.

I underestimated the sheer number of ancestors I have, and after having spent a fair amount of time on the site, I only had traced back through the Warren name. Each new generation opened up two new branches, and it was overwhelming to try to investigate all of them.

I discovered that my family came to North America a lot earlier than I had suspected. I also discovered that many, many generations back—going back to the 11th century—one of my ancestors was named the King of Jerusalem. His brother, my great, great something uncle, was Henry II, King of England. As far as I know, no one in my family had any idea.

It is strange to look back and see where my family came from. That information hasn't changed how I think of myself, but it has given me a little perspective about who I am, where I came from, and what my family has experienced.

I hope to have some time in the future to better research the rest of my family, to get an even better idea of where I come from.

Prep for the Journey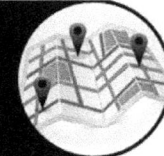

People have been interested in their family stories for a long time. Our identity is often tied to our family of origin. Throughout history, at least in much of the world, men were called by their given names and then identified as someone else's son. In Matthew, the disciples often are identified by their father. James and John are "sons of Zebedee." The other James is identified as the "son of Alphaeus." When an angel visited Joseph in Matthew 1:20, the angel called him Joseph, son of David.

What are some interesting stories about your family?

How much do you know about your family and its story?

How does that information affect the way you understand yourself?

Jesus, too, is often identified by his lineage. Sometimes he is identified as the son of Joseph, most notably when he returned to Nazareth and spoke in the synagogue, where the people took offense at his words. But Jesus is also identified as the son of David, especially when the point was to highlight his role as Messiah.

Matthew took the time to document Jesus' lineage starting with Abraham. Of course, the lineage before Abraham had already been documented in the Book of Genesis, but Matthew was not simply telling us where Jesus came from, he was making a theological argument to confirm that Jesus is the Messiah, the one of whom the prophets spoke.

> What do you remember of Jesus' lineage? What does a listing of Jesus' genealogy mean to a modern worshiper?

On the Road

Read Matthew 1:1.

An account of the genealogy of Jesus the Messiah, the son of David, the son of Abraham.

Matthew began by making two important religious and political points about Jesus. We might think that there was no reason to mention that Jesus is the son of David and the son of Abraham. Knowing that Jesus is the son of David already establishes that he is the son of Abraham. We know Abraham to be the father of Isaac, and Isaac to be the father of Jacob, and Jacob to be the father of the twelve tribes of Israel. So, we might wonder why Matthew decided in the first sentence of his gospel to affirm that Jesus is the son of David and of Abraham.

Jesus' identity as the son of Abraham was an important one to the Gospel writer. It established that Jesus came from the lineage of the Jews that was begun through Abraham, the faithful follower of God. It was with Abraham that God established covenants. It was Abraham who was promised that his descendants would be of greater number than the stars of the heavens. It was Abraham who received the promise that through his people all the people of the world would be blessed.

Naming Abraham as Jesus' ancestor brings all those promises, all those covenants to mind. Abraham is the father of the entire Jewish nation. Jesus' identity as a Jew was important to Matthew, and it continues to be important today.

Jesus' identity as son of David was also important to the Gospel writer. While the naming of Abraham established Jesus' religious identity, the naming of David established Jesus' political identity. It was David who finally established a unified Israel, bringing all of the tribes together under one leader. David was venerated as the greatest

> Would Jesus' lineage have been more or less important in the years after Jesus' resurrection, especially as the Gospels were being written? Why?

> How are Jesus' identities as "son of Abraham," and "son of David" different? What do you think each title meant to the Jews of Matthew's day? What do those titles mean to you?

king in the history of the Jewish people. And, maybe most notably, the prophets said that an ancestor of David would establish the kingdom of God's people forever.

Jesus' identity as the son of David meant that he could fulfill that promise. Jesus will re-establish the kingdom of David and he will rule forever. It took a re-thinking of the ancient prophecies to understand the way the kingdom of God was being revealed, but Matthew was quick to establish Jesus as the direct descendant of the great King David.

Scenic Route

Matthew set up the entire genealogy of Jesus in three sections. Each section is an important chapter in the history of the Jewish people, and each section has 14 generations.

The first section is the period from Abraham to David, the second is the period from David to the Babylonian Exile, and the third is the period between the Exile and Jesus' birth. Matthew emphasized the balance in God's plan as he pointed out the equal number of generations in each of these important chapters in the history of the Jewish people.

> What do you find of interest in Matthew's record of Jesus' genealogy?

Modern readers might see much of this passage as being rather monotonous, but there are a few important disruptions that make a theological and a political statement about Jesus.

Read Matthew 1:5-6.
...and Salmon the father of Boaz by Rahab, and Boaz the father of Obed by Ruth, and Obed the father of Jesse, ⁶ and Jesse the father of King David.

And David was the father of Solomon by the wife of Uriah,...

Almost the entire genealogy of Jesus mentions only men. The importance of the relationship of father to son was primary in the world view at that time. Women were thought to be mere vessels to carry the child, so they were often excluded from the lists of ancestors.

> When you look back at your family history, what roles have the women played? If Matthew were to record your genealogy, which of your female ancestors would he include?

But in Matthew's genealogy, three women are mentioned as ancestors of Jesus within only two verses. These three women each had a considerable amount of baggage in their lives. There could have been a great deal of shame, depending upon one's world view, for being the descendant of any of these three women. And yet, here they are, boldly named within Matthew's genealogy of Jesus when he could have simply left out their names.

First is Rahab. She lived in the city wall of Jericho and hid the Hebrew spies when they were investigating the land before the Joshua led the invasion of the Promised Land. She was, according to scripture, a prostitute. That profession was not viewed with the same stigma as it is in modern society, but it is remarkable that Matthew made a point to let the reader know that Jesus was descended from a prostitute who was not a daughter of Abraham, but a member of a foreign nation. This woman was kind and helpful to the Israelites. Because of her kindness, she and her family were spared when Jericho fell and become part of the Hebrew nation.

Second is Ruth. Ruth is worthy of our praise. She was faithful to her mother-in-law, even when it meant leaving her own family behind and going to a strange land. She followed her mother-in-law's instructions and ensured their survival by finding a new husband who would provide for them both. Again, modern readers might consider this story as an old sexist fairy tale, but the need for a male relative to care for Ruth and Naomi was very real.

Ruth was not an Israelite. She was from Moab. If Matthew had wanted to emphasize the purity of Jesus' heritage as a Jew, he would certainly not have mentioned Ruth in this list. Instead, he went out of his way to mention Ruth as Jesus' ancestor.

Finally, there is Bathsheba. She isn't mentioned by name, but Matthew points out that Solomon was David's son by the wife of Uriah. David had seen and desired the wife of one of his warriors, Uriah, while the troops were off fighting. Scripture suggests that David should have been with them, but he had stayed at the palace.

David sent for Bathsheba, knowing she was married. Women had no rights, so she could hardly have refused the king. As a result of their liaison, Bathsheba conceived a child. David tried to cover up his sin by having Uriah sent home so he could be with his wife. That way everyone would think the child was Uriah's. Uriah refused to return to his wife, righteously saying that he would not go home while his fellow soldiers were sleeping on the battlefield. David then effectively murdered Uriah by having the troops abandon him on the battlefield.

It is hard to imagine a story that could make David look much worse than this one. He took someone else's wife, committed adultery, and then murdered his mistress' husband. Again, if Matthew was trying to make Jesus' line look pure, he could easily have omitted a reference to Bathsheba. But Matthew presented the lineage with its baggage.

There is a fourth woman in the genealogy, listed in verse 16: "... and Jacob the father of Joseph the husband of Mary, of whom Jesus was born, who is called the Messiah." It is notable to remember that, even though we have great esteem for Mary, she probably lived with much of the shame that the other women mentioned in this genealogy did because she was found to be pregnant before she was married. We understand that pregnancy as a gift from the Holy Spirit, but imagine what the people in her day would have thought about her.

> How would you feel to discover that you were descended from someone who had a questionable background? How likely would you be to share that part of your family's history?

> In a nation where the majority of people can trace their ancestors to a different country, how important is Ruth's status as a foreigner? Why was it important enough for Matthew to note it?

> What purpose did including the reference to Bathsheba serve? What references in your own history would you like to omit?

> What was Matthew trying to convey by naming these women in Jesus' genealogy? What would it have meant for a Jew during Jesus' time to read about these women? What might it have meant for a Gentile? What does it mean for us?

While we might think that Mary is the one woman in Matthew's list who didn't have baggage, she certainly would have been treated poorly by others for the shame of being unwed and pregnant.

Workers Ahead

To Matthew, the family from which Jesus came was very important. I have seen charts of Jesus' lineage that trace both Joseph and Mary to King David. For Matthew it was important that Joseph be established as a direct descendant of David because he was Jesus' "father." For others it was important for Mary to be a direct descendant of David because, as Jesus' mother, she was the only biological human parent Jesus had.

How do we make sense of this, and what does it mean to our faith? Matthew certainly wanted to point out Jesus' connection to the ancient Israelite people and his claim to the throne of David. Both of these are important to us as we make sense of the way Jesus fulfilled the prophecies that were written about him in the Hebrew Scriptures. The ways in which Jesus is connected to those prophecies and the stories of the ancient people show us that the Old and New Testaments are part of a continuing story, instead of two separate accounts of God's work in the world.

I think the information about the flawed and broken people within Jesus' genealogy can be instructive to us as well. Jesus didn't come from perfect people. Even King David was a deeply flawed person. The stories about the women that could have been shameful to some people are stories of triumph instead. These are women who overcame their circumstances. Not only did they become prominent members of their society, they also became ancestors of the very Messiah!

As we apply these examples to our lives, we will find that God can use us despite our flaws, scars, and baggage. God can transform even our flaws into good for the kingdom of God. We recognize that no person is perfect, but at the same time, we often expect ourselves to be perfect, which isn't healthy.

Looking into the lineage of Jesus, we see what God can do with bad circumstances, with people's sins, and with failures. God can turn them into source of new blessings, even blessings as wonderful as the birth of the Christ.

> How is an unwed pregnant woman, especially a young teenager, treated by society today? How might you offer comfort and hope to young women in this situation?

> How do you see your life as part of a continuing story? What role does God have in that story?

> What within yourself have you thought God could not use? How does the realization that God can make good things out of bad circumstances affect your perspective of others? How does it affect your perspective of yourself?

In the Rear View

Matthew chose to begin the story of Jesus by sharing his ancestry. Make no mistake, the ancestry of Jesus tells a story. It tells from where he came and whose lives led to the birth of the Messiah. The account follows a path through some surprising places.

We may wonder why Matthew chose to include stories of people who were not shining examples of Israelite purity. But isn't that the very story of the gospel itself? Out of impurity, out of sin, God was making a way for there to be purity and a life free from sin.

In a way, the story of Jesus' lineage is the story of the gospel in short form. There was a lot of good in the history of the people, but there were also a lot of mistakes, a lot of poor choices, and sometimes downright evil. But even out of all that, God made a way for there to be redemption.

Thanks be to God for these awesome acts of creating new life out of death!

> How can you help the world to understand the possibility for redemption, even for those who are broken?

Travel Log

Day 1:
Take a moment to reflect on your family lineage. Note the source of some of your characteristics. From whom did you inherit your eyes, your height? How about your hair, or even your sense of humor? What does your family tell you about who you are?

Day 2:
Take a moment to write down ways in which you have chosen to go a different way than your family before you did. Why did you make those choices? Maybe you moved away from your hometown, maybe your family had a business or trade that you decided not to join. Maybe that decision was something trivial—or something profound. What have you done to differentiate yourself from your family?

Day 3:

Think about Jesus' lineage. What would make Matthew choose to start Jesus' line with Abraham? How is Abraham the source of the faith that we share? Write a letter to Abraham, perhaps expressing gratitude for his role in the faith, perhaps asking questions of why he did things he did.

Day 4:

Think about David. How was he the kind of man God wanted him to be? How did David fail in his role as king? in his faithfulness to God?

What would you like to say to David? What would you like to ask him about? Take a moment to write your words to him.

Day 5:
The women in Jesus' line were very important to Matthew. In a time when women were not mentioned often, he placed three of them within the first few verses of his Gospel.

Choose either Rahab, Ruth, or Bathsheba. Imagine what life would have been like for them. Write a story about how they might have reacted to being included in the lineage of the Messiah.

Day 6:
Matthew arranged his genealogy of Jesus into three distinct periods. Each period was balanced with 14 generations.

Look back at your family or at your personal life. How would you arrange your life or your family into different periods? What are some pivotal events that would mark the difference between of one period and another?

Write a letter to yourself, either from yourself in another period of your life or from a family member in another period of your family history. What advice would you or that family member offer?

Day 7:
Mary is the final woman mentioned in Jesus' line. As the study has already mentioned, although we tend to think of Mary very highly, she may well have been ostracized by family and friends when she became pregnant.

Make some notes as to the feelings you might have experienced if you had found yourself in Mary's situation. How would you feel if you knew, generations later, that your name would be remembered as one of purity and of greatness instead of as an unwed teenage mother?

You Want Me to Do What?

Scripture for lesson: Matthew 1:20-21*a*, 24*a*; 2:1-5, 8-9, 12-23

Written by Chris Warren

It doesn't seem like all that long ago that I was preparing for the birth of my firstborn child. She is fourteen years old now, but I still remember the anticipation, the excitement, the wonder as God was creating something new. Every week as the due date for our daughter approached, Joy (my wife) and I became more and more excited. When that date came and went, our nervousness went through the roof!

We kept a bag packed and in the truck at all times. About midway through the ninth month, Joy and I rarely went anywhere separately.

And then the day finally came: Our daughter was born. She was born in the most modern of hospitals surrounded by doctors and nurses. She was quickly taken to the nursery where they assessed her health and cleaned her. In the midst of all that, I understood how fragile new life was and how much I wanted to protect her from the difficulties of the world.

Joseph almost immediately had to fear for his baby's life. While I tend to think that our desires, even some of our emotions, were similar, Joseph and I had very different experiences of bringing a child into the world. When I think of what I would have done to make the world safe for my daughter, I can only empathize with Joseph, who was warned that the baby's life was in danger, which is unimaginable to me.

Prep for the Journey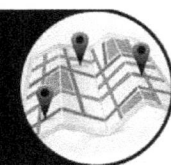

Matthew and Luke are the only Gospels that contain information about Jesus' birth and early years, and they give very different accounts. In Luke's Gospel, an angel delivered a message to Mary. In Matthew's account, Joseph also received messages from God, but the messages came in the form of dreams. In the first dream, an angel told Joseph that he should not be afraid to take Mary as his wife because the child she carried was from God.

How is having a baby different now than it was in the distant past? What things are the same as they were many years ago?

What stories do you have from your family about caring for an infant or keeping a baby safe?

What stories do you know about your own birth?

Read Matthew 1:20-21a, 24a.

An angel of the Lord appeared to him in a dream and said, "Joseph, son of David, do not be afraid to take Mary as your wife, for the child conceived in her is from the Holy Spirit. ²¹ She will bear a son, and you are to name him Jesus…²⁴ When Joseph awoke from sleep, he did as the angel of the Lord commanded him.

Matthew is the only Gospel that speaks about the visit of the Magi from the east. Most scholars think this visit was about two years after Jesus' birth. In Matthew's account, the family was apparently still living in Bethlehem when the Magi, or wise men, came to worship Jesus.

On the Road

The Magi caused quite an uproar when they came to find the newborn king of the Jews. According to the *New Interpreter's Study Bible*, some scholars think the Magi were from Parthia, an eastern enemy of Rome. Because Herod was a Roman ruler, the entry of these enemies into his kingdom, much less into his own palace, was more than enough to make him nervous. But their message about the birth of a new king threatened the political stability of the area under Herod's rule. At that time, Roman subjects were expected to worship the emperor. Worshiping a different ruler indicated to Herod that problems were on the horizon.

How would you feel if people from a foreign country came to tell you that a new ruler for your nation had been born? Why might you feel that way?

Read Matthew 2:1-5.

In the time of King Herod, after Jesus was born in Bethlehem of Judea, wise men from the East came to Jerusalem, ² asking, "Where is the child who has been born king of the Jews? For we observed his star at its rising, and have come to pay him homage." ³ When King Herod heard this, he was frightened, and all Jerusalem with him; ⁴ and calling together all the chief priests and scribes of the people, he inquired of them where the Messiah was to be born. ⁵ They told him, "In Bethlehem of Judea; for so it has been written by the prophet.

We may think that the people would have been happy to learn about the birth of a new king, but without the vision to see this new king as the promised Messiah, the people instead became afraid of what a struggle for power within the realm would bring. Herod is often thought of as a tyrant, especially from the biblical accounts, but he was a powerful ruler who brought a lot of stability to the land by keeping a close alliance with Rome. Add to this fact that Herod had rebuilt the Temple, and we can see how important he was to the people closest to him in Jerusalem. These folks didn't know whether a new king would be better for them or not.

How do you think the Magi felt about their visit at Herod's palace? Why?

Why are people often hesitant to leave oppressive situations? How do you think these factors influenced the people's feelings about a new king?

> If you had been one of Herod's advisers, what might you have told him to do about the visit from the Magi?

Read Matthew 2:8-9, 12.

Then he [Herod] sent them to Bethlehem, saying, "Go and search diligently for the child; and when you have found him, bring me word so that I may also go and pay him homage." ⁹ When they had heard the king, they set out; and there, ahead of them, went the star that they had seen at its rising, until it stopped over the place where the child was.... ¹² And having been warned in a dream not to return to Herod, they left for their own country by another road.

Fearing for the survival of his kingdom, and likely his life, Herod was trying to be very politically savvy by accommodating the Magi's request for information. By finding out where this new king was to have been born, and then asking the Magi to return with information so that he could also go and worship him, Herod gave the impression that he was "in the know" about the entire situation. His cooperation also implied that he would be supportive of this new king.

Once the Magi were on their way, however, Herod decided to seek out the child and have him killed before he became a threat. Joseph received a warning from an angel, or Jesus would have been among the children Herod found.

Read Matthew 2:13-15.

Now after they [wise men] had left, an angel of the Lord appeared to Joseph in a dream and said, "Get up, take the child and his mother, and flee to Egypt, and remain there until I tell you; for Herod is about to search for the child, to destroy him." ¹⁴ Then Joseph got up, took the child and his mother by night, and went to Egypt, ¹⁵ and remained there until the death of Herod. This was to fulfill what had been spoken by the Lord through the prophet, "Out of Egypt I have called my son."

> What threatens you? To what lengths are you willing to go to stop the threat?

The tragedy of this chapter reaches new depths with these next verses. While our modern world is not immune to overwhelming acts of violence, it is unusual for those acts to be specifically against children under the age of two. Yet this is exactly what we hear from the Gospel writer as we learn of Herod's response to the threat against his power.

Read Matthew 2:16-18.

When Herod saw that he had been tricked by the wise men, he was infuriated, and he sent and killed all the children in and around Bethlehem who were two years old or under, according to the time that he had learned from the wise men. ¹⁷ Then was fulfilled what had been spoken through the prophet Jeremiah:

> This is one of the most distressing passages in the Bible. How do you cope with the tragedy depicted here?

¹⁸ "A voice was heard in Ramah,
  wailing and loud lamentation,
Rachel weeping for her children;
  she refused to be consoled, because they are no more."

The unthinkable happened. Herod decided to assure his own power and the power of his own line of kings. He was willing to spill the blood of many innocent children in the hope that he would also be killing the one child who might have the ability to replace him as king.

Artistic representations of this moment in history are heartbreaking. They depict children being ripped from their mothers' arms while soldiers are killing innocents in the background. It is brutal. It is overwhelming. But it is the way Herod chose to try to keep his power.

Scenic Route

The parallels between these passages and the rest of the biblical narrative are striking. Once again God has taken the history of the people and has presented it in a new way. It is a way that tells a new story of redemption in Jesus Christ while still maintaining ties to the most important stories in the Old Testament.

Jesus is the one child who was saved out of many when there was a declaration to kill all the children. We are reminded of the story of Moses, the one boy who was saved out of the hands of the Egyptians while they were killing all the male babies. God chose Moses as an infant to be the one who would deliver the people from their lives of slavery and oppression in Egypt. Jesus was the one chosen to be the redeemer of the people from their slavery to sin and death.

The prophecy in verse 15 that says, "Out of Egypt I have called my son," is a reference to the calling of the people out of slavery in Egypt. The Messiah walked the same path as the ancient Israelites as he was also called from Egypt into the land of Canaan.

There is also a tie to the Babylonian Exile. The quote in verse 18, which comes from the Book of Jeremiah, is about the destruction of the city of Jerusalem and the loss of life when the people fell to Babylon. The people were seemingly destroyed in that moment. The quote fits aptly with the slaughter of the innocents in Matthew. At the same time it reminds the people that, although they were destroyed as a people back in the time of the Babylonian Exile, they can also be rebuilt. This coming child, the baby spared from Herod's wrath, was the one who would rebuild the people of Israel.

It is beautiful how Matthew tied the story of Jesus' birth with some of the most important stories in the Old Testament (the only scripture Jesus knew). Matthew's record continues the story of ancient Israel by showing how it is repeated in the life of Jesus. In the new story, however, overcoming slavery and bondage will be eternal.

With what modern day situations might this story be comparable? Why are they happening? What is our responsibility to those who are suffering?

In her novel *Christ the Lord: Out of Egypt*, Anne Rice imagines Jesus' life as he grows from a boy into a man. Jesus is deeply affected when, as a teenager, he learns that many children died at Herod's hands because of him. Have you ever considered this idea? What images or thoughts come to your mind?

Have you ever contemplated the similarities in Jesus' story as a baby and the story of the baby Moses? What strikes you as interesting in that comparison?

Matthew used the scripture from Jeremiah just before the Babylonian Exile to relate to the slaughter of the innocents in Herod's time. How were those events similar? How were they different?

What would you say overall about the way Matthew uses the Old Testament scripture in the story of Jesus' birth?

Workers Ahead

It must have been difficult for Joseph and Mary to realize that their lives and that of their son were actually in danger. They likely felt panic, fear, and even anger. We all want what is best for our families. Imagining ourselves in Joseph's place, running from the king of his own people, helps us to understand just how difficult it must have been to be the parents of the Messiah.

Read Matthew 2:19-23.

When Herod died, an angel of the Lord suddenly appeared in a dream to Joseph in Egypt and said, [20] "Get up, take the child and his mother, and go to the land of Israel, for those who were seeking the child's life are dead." [21] Then Joseph got up, took the child and his mother, and went to the land of Israel. [22] But when he heard that Archelaus was ruling over Judea in place of his father Herod, he was afraid to go there. And after being warned in a dream, he went away to the district of Galilee. [23] There he made his home in a town called Nazareth, so that what had been spoken through the prophets might be fulfilled, "He will be called a Nazorean."

While there may not currently be a decree issued to kill young children, thousands of children around the world suffer and/or die each year from hunger, neglect, war, and the lack of life's basic necessities. Some of those children may even live near you. How is God calling you to step out in faith to care for those children and others who are suffering?

Like Joseph's, sometimes our journeys are difficult. They may even be dangerous. Most of the time we do not clearly hear God telling us what to do. We may not know exactly what God's purposes are for our lives, but we can follow Joseph's example by listening for God's word and doing our best to fulfill it.

> When has God led you on a path that you didn't understand?

> When have you been able to look back in your life and see God's leading hand, even when the journey was confusing at the time?

In the Rear View

In today's lesson we explored what was a terrible ordeal in Joseph's life. He had already been through the shock of having a baby with his wife before they were married. The shock was intensified by knowing just how much God had entrusted to him with such a special baby.

Then when life was beginning to settle down, the wise men came, alerting Herod to the presence of the newborn king. Joseph and Mary suddenly faced greater danger than before Jesus was born. Now their very lives were in jeopardy. Joseph took his family and fled to a foreign land until it was safe for them return.

God appeared to Joseph in dreams, guiding Joseph and his family to safety. While we likely envy Joseph in that God's plans for him were so explicit, we need to be open to God's voice in our lives. We need to listen for God's guidance, recognize it when it comes, and then do our best to live out God's plans for us. Joseph is a model of faithfulness to God for that time and for our time.

> What do you think was Joseph's greatest strength? How have you demonstrated similar strengths in times of crisis?

Travel Log

Day 1:
   Record your fears about your journey with God. Where has God been leading you that you have been afraid to go? How have you been avoiding God's voice? What do you plan to do about it?

Day 2:
   The tragedy of loss of life, even the loss of innocent children, is not something that has gone away over time. In our world right now, many innocent people suffer at the hands of unrighteous persons who are in power. Glance through news articles and identify groups of innocent people who are being persecuted. What do you think God has to say about these innocent ones? What can you do about such persecution? Make some notes as to how you can address these issues.

Day 3:

The study mentioned a novel imagining Jesus' reaction when, as a young man, he realized that so many children died because Herod was trying to kill him. Write a response to this idea. What if you found out that many had lost their lives because someone was trying to hurt you? How would you process this information?

Day 4:

The parallels between the Old Testament stories of redemption and the story of Jesus' birth bringing redemption to the world are striking. Choose either the story of Moses and the basket or the Babylonian Exile and its parallel in the story we read this week. Write about how those parallels change your perspective of the Gospel story.

Day 5:
   The return to the land of Israel was all about timing. Sometimes we want things, and we believe that God wants those things for us, but we have to wait for the right timing.
   Take a moment to write about something you have been awaiting. How is God preparing you for this event? How can you be patient and wait for God's timing?

Day 6:
   In the Gospel of Matthew, Joseph is the one who receives messages from God, but in Luke, Mary receives the messages. Consider how the recipients make the story seem different. Journal about how you receive or hope to receive messages from God in your own life.

Day 7:
This series of studies has been about prophecy and its fulfillment in Jesus. Write down a few things you think about how prophecy was fulfilled in Christ. How do the words from the ancient Israelites affect the way you read the words of the Gospel today? How do they influence your faith in Christ?

www.ingramcontent.com/pod-product-compliance
Lightning Source LLC
Chambersburg PA
CBHW081501040426
42446CB00016B/3350